SCHOLASTIC

National Curriculum
MATHS
TEXTBOOK

Year 2

Key Stage 1

NATIONAL CURRICULUM
TEXTBOOKS

National Curriculum
MATHS
TEXTBOOK

Scholastic Education, an imprint of Scholastic Ltd
Book End, Range Road, Witney, Oxfordshire, OX29 0YD
Registered office: Westfield Road, Southam,
Warwickshire CV47 0RA
www.scholastic.co.uk

© 2016, Scholastic Ltd

1 2 3 4 5 6 7 8 9   6 7 8 9 0 1 2 3 4 5

British Library Cataloguing-in-Publication Data
A catalogue record for this book is available from the British Library.

ISBN 978-1407-16020-7

Printed in Italy by STIGE – Turin

Author Ann Montague-Smith

Consultant Paul Hollin

Editorial Rachel Morgan, Jenny Wilcox, Mark Walker, Mary Nathan, Margaret Eaton, Kate Baxter, Janette Ratcliffe and Julia Roberts

Design Oxford Designers & Illustrators

Cover Design Scholastic Design Team, Nicolle Thomas and Neil Salt

Cover Illustration Shutterstock / © VIGE.CO

Illustration Tom Heard, The Bright Agency

Every effort has been made to trace copyright holders for the works reproduced in this book, and the publishers apologise for any inadvertent omissions.

Contents

Contents

Fractions

Measurement

Geometry

Statistics

How to use this book

Introduction

This book provides information and varied examples, activities and questions in a clear and consistent format, covering the National Curriculum for Mathematics for this age group.

I give tips to help you!

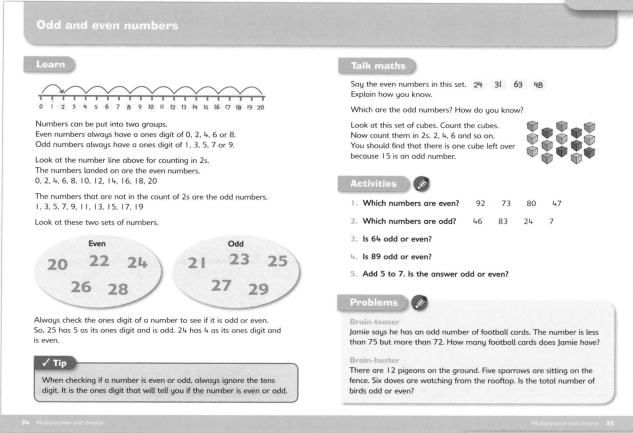

Odd and even numbers

Learn

Numbers can be put into two groups.
Even numbers always have a ones digit of 0, 2, 4, 6 or 8.
Odd numbers always have a ones digit of 1, 3, 5, 7 or 9.

Look at the number line above for counting in 2s.
The numbers landed on are the even numbers.
0, 2, 4, 6, 8, 10, 12, 14, 16, 18, 20

The numbers that are not in the count of 2s are the odd numbers.
1, 3, 5, 7, 9, 11, 13, 15, 17, 19

Look at these two sets of numbers.

Even
20 22 24 26 28

Odd
21 23 25 27 29

Always check the ones digit of a number to see if it is odd or even.
So, 25 has 5 as its ones digit and is odd. 24 has 4 as its ones digit and is even.

✓ Tip

When checking if a number is even or odd, always ignore the tens digit. It is the ones digit that will tell you if the number is even or odd.

Talk maths

Say the even numbers in this set. 24 31 63 48
Explain how you know.

Which are the odd numbers? How do you know?

Look at this set of cubes. Count the cubes.
Now count them in 2s. 2, 4, 6 and so on.
You should find that there is one cube left over because 15 is an odd number.

Activities

1. Which numbers are even? 92 73 80 47
2. Which numbers are odd? 46 83 24 7
3. Is 64 odd or even?
4. Is 89 odd or even?
5. Add 5 to 7. Is the answer odd or even?

Problems

Brain-teaser
Jamie says he has an odd number of football cards. The number is less than 75 but more than 72. How many football cards does Jamie have?

Brain-buster
There are 12 pigeons on the ground. Five sparrows are sitting on the fence. Six doves are watching from the rooftop. Is the total number of birds odd or even?

Keep some blank or squared paper handy for notes and calculations!

Structure

- **Learn** – examples and explanations of the mathematical area in focus.
- **Tips** – short and simple advice to aid understanding.
- **Talk maths** – focused activities that encourage verbal practice.
- **Activities** – a focused range of questions to practise skills learned.
- **Problems** – word problems requiring mathematics to be used in context.

* Note that Tips and Talk maths sections are not present in single-page units.

Counting in steps

Learn

We can count in steps on a number line. Follow these counts with your finger.

Count in 2s.

Count in 5s.

Count in 10s.

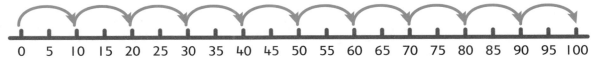

When you count in steps, all the steps must be the same. Continue to count in 3s on this number line.

Look at this number line.

Copy the last number line and mark counting in 2s from 0 using arrows. Which numbers are visited by both 2s and 5s? Why do you think that is?

✓ Tip

Learn counting in 2s to 10 by heart: 2, 4, 6, 8, 10. This will make counting in steps over 20 easier for you.

Say these counts aloud.

What do you notice about the last count?

0	2	4	6	8	10	12	14	16	18	20
0	3	6	9	12	15	18	21	24	27	30
0	5	10	15	20	25	30	35	40	45	50
0	10	20	30	40	50	60	70	80	90	100
6	16	26	36	46	56	66	76	86	96	106

Activities

1. **These counts go backwards. Copy and complete the sequences and write the missing numbers.**

   a. 20, 18, 16, _14_, _12_, _10_, 8   b. 18, 15, _12_, _9_, _6_, 3, 0

2. **Copy and complete the sequences and write the missing numbers.**

   a. 20, 30, 40, _50_, _60_, _70_   b. 35, 30, 25, _20_, _15_, _10_

3. **Start at 4. Count forward in steps of 10. Write down all the numbers below 100. The first two numbers have been done for you.**

   4, 14

Problems

Brain-teaser
There are nine pairs of shoes in the cupboard.
How many shoes are there altogether?

Brain-buster
Tom puts 10p in his money box every week. How many weeks will it take for him to save £1?

Reading and writing numbers to at least 100

Learn

These are all 2-digit numbers.

| 10 | 24 | 31 | 76 | 89 |

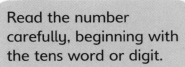

Read the number carefully, beginning with the tens word or digit.

Read them aloud.

Here are the ones words.

one	two	three	four	five	six	seven	eight	nine
1	2	3	4	5	6	7	8	9

These number words come next.

ten	eleven	twelve	thirteen	fourteen	fifteen
10	11	12	13	14	15

sixteen	seventeen	eighteen	nineteen
16	17	18	19

Here are the tens words.

ten	twenty	thirty	forty	fifty	sixty	seventy	eighty	ninety
10	20	30	40	50	60	70	80	90

Now we can put the ones words and the tens words together to make other numbers.

21	34	63	95
twenty-one	thirty-four	sixty-three	ninety-five

 Tip

When writing a 2-digit number in words, remember the hyphen: twenty-nine

Talk maths

Read these numbers aloud.

| thirty-one | fifty-six | ninety-seven | eighty-one | seventy |

Now say these.

| 47 | 81 | 72 | 19 | 44 |

Activities

1. **Read the number words. Write the number.**

 a. fifty-three **b.** ninety-nine **c.** six

 d. thirty-four **e.** twenty-two **f.** one hundred

2. **Now write these numbers in words.**

 a. 81 **b.** 14 **c.** 62 **d.** 38 **e.** 90 **f.** 47

Problems

Brain-teaser
John does his homework. He writes some numbers in words.
Which ones are correct?

a. fourty-six **b.** ninety-eight **c.** twenty-one **d.** fifty-six

Brain-buster
Lucy writes an even number between 56 and 60 in words.
What could it be?

Comparing and ordering numbers

Look at the number 18. We can say the number that is one more than 18. It is 19. We can say the number that is one less than 18. It is 17.

When comparing numbers, look at the tens digit first.

tens	ones
3	6

tens	ones
2	9

3 tens is greater than 2 tens. So **36** is greater than **29**.

If both tens digits are the same, look at the ones digit. **23** is greater than 21.

> < means **is less than**

> > means **is greater than**

> = means **is equal to**

These number sentences are true.

48 > 39

82 < 94

11 − 5 < 15

7 + 8 = 18 − 3

From smallest number to largest:

13   15   27   93

smallest   largest

From largest number to smallest:

93   27   15   13

largest   smallest

We can order 2-digit numbers from smallest to largest or from largest to smallest.

✓ Tip

Remember, always look at the tens digits first. This will help you to decide which number is larger. If both numbers have the same tens digit, look at the ones digit. Now you can decide which is the larger number.

Talk maths

Look at these number sentences and read them aloud.

36 > 29   29 < 43

They read: 36 is larger than 29, and 29 is smaller than 43. We can order these numbers from smallest to largest or the other way round.

Here are the numbers ordered smallest to largest: 29, 36, 43.
Here are the numbers ordered the other way around, largest to smallest: 43, 36, 29. Say the numbers aloud in each order.

Activities

Complete the activities below, then read each number sentence aloud.

1. Copy these number sentences, and write <, >, or = to make them true.

   a. 64 ___ 73

   b. 13 + 7 ___ 2

   c. 45 ___ 44

   d. 33 − 7 = ___ + 21

2. Write these numbers in order, starting with the smallest number.

   64   91   37   72   59

Problems

Brain-teaser
Delun has 34 sweets, Iha has 43 sweets and Jamie has 24 sweets. Who has the fewest sweets?

Brain-buster
Jon has fewer than 50 sweets but more than each of the three children in the Brain-teaser. How many sweets could Jon have?

Recognising place value in 2-digit numbers

Learn

2-digit numbers are made from a tens digit and a ones digit.

A 2-digit number can also be made on an abacus.

Count the tens on the abacus to give you the tens number.

Ten, twenty, thirty.

Now count the ones on the abacus to give you the ones number.

One, two, three, four, five.

The abacus shows 35.

Here is another abacus. Read the number.

5 tens and 4 ones... it's 54!

Now draw an abacus and show 37.

✓ Tip

Try drawing your own abacus to help you to read a number. This abacus shows 23.

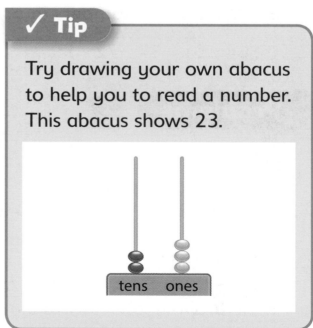

Talk maths

Here are some numbers made with tens and ones.

Say each number aloud.   30 and 5   40 and 6   70 and 8

We can write these using just one digit
for the tens and one digit for the ones.   35   46   78

Try saying some other numbers aloud and challenge a
partner to write them.

Activities

1. Write the 2-digit number
   for this abacus.

2. Copy this abacus and
   show 51 on it.

3. Look at these numbers. Write the number with the largest tens
   digit and circle it. Write the number with the smalled ones digit
   and underline it.

   45   26   61   53

Problems

Darina    Mina

Brain-teaser

How many more is on Darina's
abacus than on Mina's?

Brain-buster

Tamsin shows 74 on an abacus. She adds one more ring to the tens.
Then she adds three more rings to the ones. What number does the
abacus show now?

Showing numbers in different ways

Learn

Numbers can be shown in different ways.

Here are all the numbers from 1 to 100 on a hundred square.

1	2	3	4	5	6	7	8	9	10
11	12	13	14	15	16	17	18	19	20
21	22	23	24	25	26	27	28	29	30
31	32	33	34	35	36	37	38	39	40
41	42	43	44	45	46	47	48	49	50
51	52	53	54	55	56	57	58	59	60
61	62	63	64	65	66	67	68	69	70
71	72	73	74	75	76	77	78	79	80
81	82	83	84	85	86	87	88	89	90
91	92	93	94	95	96	97	98	99	100

What is the number that is one before 100?

It's 99!

Look at the hundred square above.
Count along the top row.
These are the numbers from 1 to 10.

Now count down the last column in tens.
These are the tens numbers from 10 to 100.

Count along the top row from 1 to 5, then count down the 5 column:
5, 15, 25, 35, 45, 55, 65, 75, 85, 95.

You can also use a number line to show where a number is.

The arrow points to where 55 belongs.

Talk maths

Look at this number line.

20   ↑   ↑   30

The first arrow is halfway along the line.
This means that the number is 25.

What number is the second arrow pointing to?
This number is greater than 25 and less than 30.
It is nearer to 30 than to 25.

Discuss with a partner how you know the answer.

Activities

1. **Look carefully at the number line. Draw the number line and mark where you estimate the number 43 is.**

    40   50

2. **Look at the hundred square.**

    a. Which number is represented by the ● ?

    b. Which number is represented by the ■ ?

    c. Which number is represented by the ▲ ?

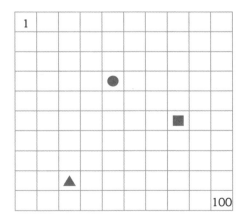

Problems

40   50

Brain-teaser

Peter draws a number line. He marks in 40 and 50. He asks Jake to estimate where 42 is. Copy the line and write in your estimate of where 42 is.

Using place value and number facts to solve problems

Look at this number sentence. $6 + 3 = 9$

We can use this number fact to solve $60 + 30$.
If $6 + 3 = 9$, then $60 + 30 = 90$.

Let's try a subtraction. What about $40 - ? = 10$

We know that $4 - 3 = 1$.

Can you use this to work out the missing number?

Think about the number facts that you know using ones.

✓ **Tip**

So if the question is $60 - ? = 20$, try $6 - 4 = 2$ to help you.

Another way to solve $40 - ? = 10$ is to use a number line.

You can also solve this by counting up from 10 to 40, in tens. Check how many tens you count. Counting up from 10, we would count 20, 30, 40. That's 3 tens, so the answer is 30.

Now addition. Look at this calculation.

$30 + ? = 50$

You can use a number line to solve this by counting up from 30 to 50.

So $30 + 20 = 50$.

And of course, we could have used $3 + 2 = 5$ to work out this answer.

Talk maths

Count along these number lines, saying the missing numbers to answer the questions.

20 + ? = 60

20   60

80 − ? = 40

40   80

70 − 10 = ?

10   70

Activities

23/4

1. **Copy these number sentences and solve them using number facts.**

   a. 50 − ? = 40   b. 20 + ? = 70   c. 90 − ? = 10

   d. 70 − ? = 30   e. 30 + ? = 100   f. 40 + ? = 90

Problems

Brain-teaser
Tom has 40 marbles. Jake has 70 marbles.
How many more marbles has Jake than Tom?

Brain-buster
Sally has 30 beads and Jane has 40 beads.
They want to make a necklace of 90 beads.
How many more beads do they need?

Addition and subtraction facts to 20 and related facts to 100

Learn

Here are some number facts that you already know.

$$2 + 6 = 8$$
$$7 + 9 = 16$$
$$14 - 9 = 5$$
$$16 + 2 = 18$$

You can use facts you know to find other facts like this.

$7 + 9 = 16$	so	$16 - 7 = 9$	or	$16 - 9 = 7$
$9 + 7 = 16$	so	$16 - 9 = 7$	or	$16 - 7 = 9$

You can use that fact to work out that $27 + 9 = 36$.

Then you can work out other facts like this, using these numbers.

$$9 + 27 = 36$$
$$36 - 9 = 27$$
$$36 - 27 = 9$$

✓ Tip

Remember to use the number facts that you do know to find the answer.

Here's another fact you know.
$$15 - 6 = 9$$
So $25 - 6 = 19$.
And $25 - 16 = 9$.

Let's do one more.
$$14 + 5 = 19$$
So $34 + 5 = 39$.
And $34 + 15 = 49$.

Draw a number line and count on to check your answers.

Talk maths

You know that $9 + 6 = 15$. So $19 + 6 = 25$. And $29 + 6 = 35$.

Here are some more.

$39 + 6 = 45$ $49 + 6 = 55$

Discuss the pattern you can see with a partner.

Let's try something different.

$6 - 4 = 2$ So $16 - 4 = 12$ $26 - 14 = 12$ $36 - 24 = 12$

All these facts use your knowledge that $6 - 4 = 2$.

Activities

Copy and complete these calculations.

1. $12 + 6 = ?$ So $22 + 6 = ?$

2. $14 - 12 = ?$ So $24 - 2 = ?$

3. $9 + 6 = ?$ So $29 + 6 = ?$

4. $18 - 9 = ?$ So $38 - 9 = ?$

5. $12 + 7 = ?$ So $32 + 7 = ?$

Problems

Brain-teaser

Mike has 12 marbles and Tom has 4. They have 16 marbles altogether.
John has 22 marbles and Phil has 4. How many marbles do they have
altogether?

Brain-buster

Jade has 14 pens. She gives Sam three pens. Now
Jade has 11 pens left. Sally has 44 pens. She gives
Lin 23 pens. How many pens does Sally have now?

Adding and subtracting mentally

Learn

You know lots of number facts already.

| 4 + 5 = 9 | 9 − 7 = 2 | 12 + 6 = 18 | 20 − 7 = 13 |

You can use these number facts to help you to find other facts.

64 + 5   You can use 4 + 5 = 9 to solve this. So 64 + 5 = 69.

Let's look at   59 − 7 . Well, you know that 9 − 7 = 2. So 59 − 7 = 52.

When adding a 2-digit number and tens, count on in tens.
43 add 30 is 53, 63, 73. 43 + 30 = 73.

> Or add the 4 tens and the 3 tens in your head to make 70 then add back the 3 ones to make 73.

For subtracting tens from a 2-digit number:
36 − 10 is 26. So 36 − 20 is 16.
And 36 − 30 is 6.

To add two 2-digit numbers add the tens first then the ones. So for 51 + 33: add 50 and 30 to make 80, then the 1 and 3 to make 4. That equals 84.

Let's try a subtraction: 56 subtract 34 .
Subtract the tens first, then the ones.
We use 5 − 3 = 2 to help with subtracting the tens. 50 − 30 = 20.
And 6 − 4 = 2 can be used for subtracting the ones.
So 56 − 34 = 22.

✓ Tip

Remember when working mentally you can count on or back in ones or tens, or add or subtract the tens, and then the ones.

Talk maths

Talk through these examples with a partner.

24 + 5   We know that 4 + 5 = 9, so 24 + 5 = 29.

35 − 4   5 − 4 = 1, so 35 − 4 = 31.

54 + 20   Here it is just the tens that will change, not the ones.
We know that 5 + 2 = 7, so 50 + 20 = 70 and 54 + 20 = 74.

54 − 20   Just the tens will change here. 5 − 2 = 3, so 50 − 20 = 30
and so 54 − 20 = 34.

34 + 21   3 + 2 = 5, so 30 + 20 = 50 and 4 + 1 = 5.
Let's put those together. 34 + 21 = 55.

67 − 25   6 − 2 = 4, so 60 − 20 = 40 and 7 − 5 = 2.
Put those together. 67 − 25 = 42.

Activities

Work these calculations out mentally.

1. 46 + 3   **2.** 55 + 40   **3.** 67 − 26

4. 98 − 7   **5.** 36 + 23   **6.** 84 − 22

Problems

Brain-teaser
There are 24 swap cards in the pile. James puts another 20 swap cards
on the pile. How many swap cards are there altogether?

Brain-buster
Marta has 55 swap cards. She gives her sister 23 of her cards.
How many cards does Marta have left?

Adding and subtracting by using objects and representations

Learn

Use a mental number line to count on or back in ones to help you.

Adding 2-digit numbers and ones

54 + 7 Make the next 10, then add on the rest of the ones.

54 and 6 is 60 and 1 more is 61. So 54 + 7 = 61.

You could also use a hundred square. Find 54 then count to the next 10 (60). You have added 6.
Now count on 1 more so that 7 is added. The answer is 61.

Subtracting 2-digit numbers and ones

54 – 7 Subtract 4 to reach 50. Then subtract the remaining 3.
The answer is 47.

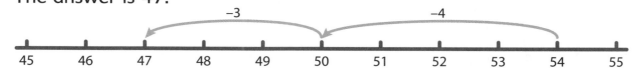

Adding a 2-digit number and tens

43 + 30 Add the tens digits first. Use a hundred square to count on.
40 + 30 is 40 and 50, 60, 70. So 40 + 30 = 70.
Add on the 3: 43 + 30 = 73

Adding two 2-digit numbers

36 + 28 Start by adding the tens.
36 + 28 ➜ 36 + 20 + 8 ➜ 56 + 8 = 64

Use a number line to help you count on the tens and ones.

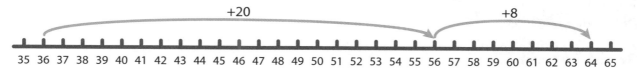

Finding the difference between two 2-digit numbers

64 – 39 Count up from 39 on a number line like this. So 64 – 39 = 25.

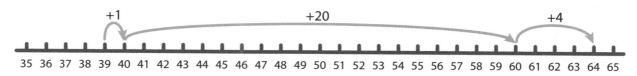

Talk maths

Look at each number sentence. Talk with a partner about how you would find the answer.

| 62 + 8 | 35 + 40 | 32 + 43 |
| 51 – 4 | 67 – 50 | 72 – 55 |

✓ Tip

Choose the best method for you. This may not be the same as your partner's.

Activities

Choose how you will find the answer. Write this out each time.

1. 63 + 8 ✓

2. 97 – 8 ✓

3. 45 + 20 ✓

4. 65 – 30 ✓

5. 47 + 21 ✓

6. 64 – 36 ✓

Problems

Brain-teaser

Tim has 63 marbles. He lends 45 marbles to Sam. How many marbles does Tim have now?

Brain-buster

Paula gave Marcus 25 sweets. She has 26 sweets left. How many sweets did Paula have before she gave some to Marcus?

Adding three 1-digit numbers

Learn

Here are some ideas for adding three 1-digit numbers.

Make a 10

| 6 + 4 + 8 | 6 + 4 is 10 | 10 + 8 is 18 |

We can also use this for 3 + 6 + 7. Put the numbers into a different order to help make 10. 3 + 7 + 6 = 10 + 6 = 16.

Look for doubles

| 7 + 7 + 4 | 7 + 7 is 14 | 14 + 4 is 18 |
| 9 + 5 + 9 | 9 + 9 is 18 | 18 + 5 can be seen as 18 + 2 + 3. |

18 + 2 = 20   20 + 3 = 23

> ### ✓ Tip
>
> Draw a number line to help you. For a subtraction that has a missing number, count on from the lower to the higher number to give the missing number. This works for addition too!

Choose the best order to add

When adding three 1-digit numbers, decide which is the best order for you to add them.

| 6 + 5 + 6 | 6 + 6 is 12 | 12 + 5 = 17 | . |

Use objects and diagrams

You can also use cubes, number lines and hundred squares to help you add three 1-digit numbers.

Talk maths

Say how you would do each of these. Remember, you are working mentally. Now work out the answer for each one. Explain how you worked.

| 5 + 5 + 6 | 3 + 9 + 3 | 4 + 8 + 7 | 9 + 2 + 6 |

 Tip

Remember when working mentally you can add three 1-digit numbers in any order.

Activities

Work the answers out mentally.

1. 2 + 2 + 4   2. 7 + 2 + 3

Choose how you will find the answer to these. Write your methods.

3. 7 + 6 + 7   4. 2 + 9 + 8   5. 5 + 2 + 9

Problems

Brain-teaser
Tom has 4 football cards. Dilshad has 6 football cards. Mark has 8 football cards. How many cards do they have in total?

Brain-buster
Mark puts down 7 marbles. Sam puts down 5 marbles. Peter puts down 8 marbles. How many marbles is that in total?

Checking calculations and missing number problems

Learn

12 + 7 = 19   Check with 19 − 12 = 7.

7 + 12 = 19   Check with 19 − 7 = 12.

This always works for addition and subtraction.

Let's try a different calculation.

23 + 5 = 28   Check with 28 − 5 = 23.

5 + 23 = 28   Check with 28 − 23 = 5.

If you work out a calculation, then you can find others.

If you start with subtraction, then you can find addition sentences in the same way.

28 − 7 = 21   Check with 7 + 21 = 28.

28 − 21 = 7   Check with 21 + 7 = 28.

If you are not sure, break the numbers down like this.

35 + 12 = 47   35 + 12 = 30 + 5 + 10 + 2 = 40 + 7 = 47

Then 12 + 35 = 47   47 − 35 = 12   47 − 12 = 35

Let's try a subtraction this time.   58 − 16 = 42

Or 58 − 16 = 50 − 10 + 8 − 6 = 42

Some questions have missing numbers. Here's a calculation to try.

25 + ? = 32

You can count up in your head or draw a number line like this.

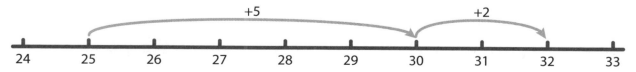

So counting on the number line gives 5 + 2 = 7. So 25 + 7 = 32.

Talk maths

We can use what we know about the link between addition and subtraction to check answers. Work out the answer to these questions. Discuss with a partner how your know the answer.

42 + 7 = 49   49 − 7 = ?   51 − 8 = 43   43 + 8 = ?

Activities

Copy this chart. Write a check calculation and then put a tick or a cross for each answer.

You can check your answers for addition by working out a subtraction using the same numbers.

	Sara's answers	Check calculations	✓ or ✗
1	12 + 7 = 19		
2	21 + 9 = 29		
3	35 − 4 = 31		
4	24 + 13 = 27		
5	54 − 23 = 31		

Problems

Brain-teaser
Vanida has 64 beads. She counts the blue beads. There are 32 blue beads. She thinks that 32 beads are red. Write a calculation to show whether Vanida is correct. Write a check calculation too.

Brain-buster
There are 35 biscuits in the tin. Yin adds another 24 biscuits. Then Yin eats 4 biscuits. Yin thinks there are now 55 biscuits in the tin. Write a check calculation to show whether Yin is correct.

Solving problems with addition and subtraction

Learn

Here are some words that you may find in problems, with their meanings.

Means add

| put together | altogether | total | how many |

Means subtract

| how many more | how many fewer | less than |

| how much change | difference between | distance between |

Some questions are asked in words:

Mary has five brothers and four sisters. How many children are there in Mary's family? Don't forget to add in Mary!
So 5 brothers + 4 sisters + 1 Mary = 5 + 4 + 1 = 10

Read this problem carefully. Think about how you would solve it.

Read the problem carefully. Look for the key words in the problem.

A box of cherries costs 65p.
How much change will I get from £1?
To solve this, subtract 65p from £1.
Don't forget to change the £1 to 100 pennies.
You could use a number line like this.

Counting up from 65 to 100 gives us 5 + 30, or 35.
So the change is 35p.

✓ Tip

Underline the key words and numbers in the problem. Then you have all the key facts.

Talk maths

Read aloud the problems. The key words and numbers are in blue.

> John is reading some comics. One comic has **45** pages and the other one has **39** pages. **How many** pages is that **altogether**?

How many and **altogether** tell us this is an add problem. So 45 + 39.

> Sarah has **14** goldfish in a fish tank. She also has **26** goldfish in the garden pond. **How many more** goldfish does Sarah need to make **50**?

To solve this problem we need to find out how many goldfish Sarah has now. So 14 + 26 = 10 + 20 + 4 + 6 = 30 + 10 = 40. Sarah has 40 goldfish. The problem asks **how many more** goldfish Sarah needs to make 50. So 50 − 40 = 10. ➡ Sarah needs 10 more goldfish.

Activities

1. There are 27 kittens and 19 puppies at the rescue centre. How many are there in total? Show your working.

2. 64 children wanted to go to the cinema. There were just 35 tickets left. How many children did not get a ticket? Show your working.

Problems

Brain-teaser
Lollies cost 10p each and ice creams cost 25p each. Josh buys one lolly and two ice creams. How much does he spend?

Brain-buster
The shop sells pencils at 10p each and pens at 35p each. Peter buys two pencils and two pens. How much change will Peter get from £1?

Multiplication and division facts for the 10-times table

Learn

These are the signs that are used in multiplication and division.

× means multiply.   **÷** means divide.

Remember the word **multiple**. It means the answer when you multiply.

So, in the 10-times table the multiples are:
0, 10, 20, 30, 40, 50, 60, 70, 80, 90, 100, 110, 120.

> All multiples in the 10-times table have a 0 ones digit.

10-times table	Dividing by 10
$1 \times 10 = 10$	$10 \div 10 = 1$
$2 \times 10 = 20$	$20 \div 10 = 2$
$3 \times 10 = 30$	$30 \div 10 = 3$
$4 \times 10 = 40$	$40 \div 10 = 4$
$5 \times 10 = 50$	$50 \div 10 = 5$
$6 \times 10 = 60$	$60 \div 10 = 6$
$7 \times 10 = 70$	$70 \div 10 = 7$
$8 \times 10 = 80$	$80 \div 10 = 8$
$9 \times 10 = 90$	$90 \div 10 = 9$
$10 \times 10 = 100$	$100 \div 10 = 10$
$11 \times 10 = 110$	$110 \div 10 = 11$
$12 \times 10 = 120$	$120 \div 10 = 12$

Which of these numbers are in the 10-times table?
    15   90   25   40

Look at the ones digit. Only if it is a 0 will it be in the 10-times table. So the answer is 90 and 40.

It is important to learn your tables so that you can remember these multiplication facts easily.

✓ Tip

If you're not sure about a fact, try a number line like this.

Counting back from 40 in tens helps you to find $40 \div 10 = 4$.

Look carefully at this set of four number sentences.
Say each number sentence.

| $10 \times 5 = 50$ | $5 \times 10 = 50$ | $50 \div 10 = 5$ | $50 \div 5 = 10$ |

All these number sentences are made from the multiplication fact
$10 \times 5 = 50$.

Now say the first number sentence below.
Use the numbers to complete the others in the set.

$9 \times 10 = 90$ $10 \times ? = 90$

$90 \div ? = 9$ $90 \div ? = 10$

Remember, if you know a multiplication sentence you can use those
numbers to make another multiplication and two division sentences.

Activities

Copy and complete these times tables fact.

1. 6×10
2. 3×10
3. 10×10
4. $50 \div 10$
4. $90 \div 10$

Problems

Brain-teaser

Jane has four packs of 10 pens. How many pens
is that in total?

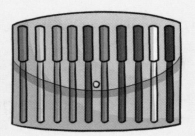

Brain-buster

Mya buys six packs of pens. Each pack has 10 pens. Mya gives two
packs of pens to her sister. How many pens does Mya have now?

Multiplication and division facts for the 2- and 5-times tables

Learn

Here is the count in 2s.

0 2 4 6 8 10 12 14 16 18 20 22 24

This count in 2s is used in the 2-times table.

And here is the count in 5s.

0 5 10 15 20 25 30 35 40 45 50 55 60

This count in 5s is used in the 5-times table.

2-times table	5-times table
$1 \times 2 = 2$	$1 \times 5 = 5$
$2 \times 2 = 4$	$2 \times 5 = 10$
$3 \times 2 = 6$	$3 \times 5 = 15$
$4 \times 2 = 8$	$4 \times 5 = 20$
$5 \times 2 = 10$	$5 \times 5 = 25$
$6 \times 2 = 12$	$6 \times 5 = 30$
$7 \times 2 = 14$	$7 \times 5 = 35$
$8 \times 2 = 16$	$8 \times 5 = 40$
$9 \times 2 = 18$	$9 \times 5 = 45$
$10 \times 2 = 20$	$10 \times 5 = 50$
$11 \times 2 = 22$	$11 \times 5 = 55$
$12 \times 2 = 24$	$12 \times 5 = 60$

Here are some facts that will help you with multiplication and division by 2, 5 and 10.

All multiples of 2 have a 0, 2, 4, 6 or 8 as their last digit.

All multiples of 5 have a 5 or 0 as their last digit.

These facts make it easy to spot multiples of numbers.

- 25 ends in 5, so it's a multiple of 5.
- 18 ends in 8, so it's a multiple of 2.
- 56 ends in 6, so it's a multiple of 2.
- 70 ends in 0 so it is a multiple of 2 and 5.

✓ Tip

If you don't know the answer, draw a number line to help you.

Talk maths

All these numbers are multiples. They belong to the 2- or 5-times table. Say the multiplication fact for each. Look at the ones digit to help you.

18   ? × ? = ?   45   ? × ? = ?   6   ? × ? = ?

25   ? × ? = ?   22   ? × ? = ?

Some multiples belong to more than one multiplication table.
10 is 1 × 10 and 2 × 5 and 5 × 2. 20 is 2 × 10 and 4 × 5 and 10 × 2.
Think of some more multiples that are in the 5- and 10-times tables.

Activities

1. **Copy each number sentence and write a multiplication fact from the 2- or 5-times table.**

   a.   35   ? × ? = 35   b.   50   ? × ? = 50

   c.   16   ? × ? = 16   d.   24   ? × ? = 24

2. **Copy and write a division fact from the 2- or 5-times table.**

   a.   6   6 ÷ ? = ?   b.   25   25 ÷ ? = ?

Problems

Brain-teaser

Ava has five boxes of raisins. Each box holds eight raisins.
How many raisins does Ava have in total?

Brain-buster

Sophie has 69 marbles. She keeps 39 marbles for herself.
She shares out the rest of the marbles between her
five sisters. How many marbles does each sister get?

Odd and even numbers

Learn

Numbers can be put into two groups.
Even numbers always have a ones digit of 0, 2, 4, 6 or 8.
Odd numbers always have a ones digit of 1, 3, 5, 7 or 9.

Look at the number line above for counting in 2s.
The numbers landed on are the even numbers.
0, 2, 4, 6, 8, 10, 12, 14, 16, 18, 20

The numbers that are not in the count of 2s are the odd numbers.
1, 3, 5, 7, 9, 11, 13, 15, 17, 19

Look at these two sets of numbers.

Always check the ones digit of a number to see if it is odd or even.
So, 25 has 5 as its ones digit and is odd. 24 has 4 as its ones digit and
is even.

✓ **Tip**

When checking if a number is even or odd, always ignore the tens
digit. It is the ones digit that will tell you if the number is even or odd.

Talk maths

Say the even numbers in this set. 24 31 63 48
Explain how you know.

Which are the odd numbers? How do you know?

Look at this set of cubes. Count the cubes.
Now count them in 2s. 2, 4, 6 and so on.
You should find that there is one cube left over
because 15 is an odd number.

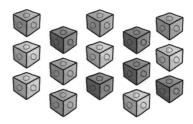

Activities

1. **Which numbers are even?**   92   73   80   47

2. **Which numbers are odd?**   46   83   24   7

3. **Is 64 odd or even?**

4. **Is 89 odd or even?**

5. **Add 5 to 7. Is the answer odd or even?**

Problems

Brain-teaser

Jamie says he has an odd number of football cards. The number is less
than 75 but more than 72. How many football cards does Jamie have?

Brain-buster

There are 12 pigeons on the ground. Five sparrows are sitting on the
fence. Six doves are watching from the rooftop. Is the total number of
birds odd or even?

Solving problems involving multiplication and division

Here is an array. It has 2 rows of spots.
Each row has 5 spots in it.

So in total there are 10 spots.

$5 \times 7 = 35$ $7 \times 5 = 35$ $35 \div 5 = 7$ $35 \div 7 = 5$

You can make arrays to show multiplication and division like this.

Look at this multiplication array.

How many rows of spots are there? How many columns of spots are there?

So 5 rows and 3 columns of spots gives 15 spots in total.
$5 \times 3 = 15$ or $3 \times 5 = 15$.

Division can be found from arrays too. Count the number of rows.
Count the number of columns.
So $15 \div 5 = 3$ and $15 \div 3 = 5$.

Draw the array for 6×2.
$12 \div 2 = 6$ and $12 \div 6 = 2$.

Now you have $6 \times 2 = 12$ and $2 \times 6 = 12$.

✓ Tip

You can draw your own array to help you to remember multiplication and division facts.

Look at this array.

How many spots are there altogether?
Say the two multiplication facts.
Say the two division facts.
This array gives 3 × 10 = 30 and 10 × 3 = 30.
30 ÷ 3 = 10 and 30 ÷ 10 = 3.

Activities

1. **Draw the array for these calculations. Write the total each time.**

   a. 5 × 2   b. 6 × 5   c. 2 × 10

2. **Now draw the array for these calculations.**
   Write two multiplication sentences for each array.
   Write two division sentences for each array.

   a. 7 × 2   b. 4 × 5   c. 3 × 10

Problems

Brain-teaser

Bethany wants to make a patio in her garden. She has 12 paving slabs.
She makes an array where one row has 6 slabs. Write two multiplication
facts for the array.

Brain-buster

Max has some counters. He makes an array with them. There are
6 counters in a row. There are 5 counters in a column. How many
counters are there altogether?

Adding numbers in any order

Learn

Look at these numbers. 5, 6, 11 We can make two addition and two subtraction sentences with these numbers.

$5 + 6 = 11$ $6 + 5 = 11$ $11 - 5 = 6$ $11 - 6 = 5$

Here are two sets.

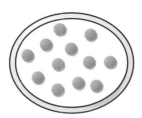 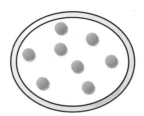

> Addition can be done in any order.
> $26 + 13 = 39$
> $13 + 26 = 39$

There are 12 in one set and 8 in the other. Now add these. Your total should be 20. So $12 + 8 = 20$.

Now do this again, this time starting with the set of 8. $8 + 12 = 20$. You have the same answer. So it does not matter which order you add in.

Now look at subtraction. $12 - 8 = 4$

Look what happens if you start with the set of 8. This would give a different answer! $8 - 12$. So the order in which you subtract **does** matter.

Activities

Look at each of these pairs of number sentences.
Which are correct, which are wrong?

1. $15 + 5 = 5 + 15$ 2. $12 - 4 = 4 - 12$ 3. $19 + 23 = 23 + 19$
4. $36 - 45 = 45 - 36$ 5. $37 + 46 = 46 - 37$

Problems

Brain-teaser

Zikri has £1. He spends 36p. He writes a number sentence to show how much money he has left, $100p - 36p = 64p$. Write an addition number sentence to show that he is correct.

Multiplying numbers in any order

Learn

Look carefully at these multiplication facts.

$2 \times 5 = 10$ $5 \times 2 = 10$

Multiplication can be done in any order.
$10 \times 5 = 50$
$5 \times 10 = 50$

We can multiply numbers in any order:
2×5 gives the same answer as 5×2.

Here are two multiplications that use the same numbers.
$3 \times 10 = 30$ and $10 \times 3 = 30$.

Now look what happens with division.
$30 \div 10 = 3$
$10 \div 30 = ?$ The answer here cannot be 3.

Division **cannot** be done in any order.

Activities

Write two multiplication sentences for each set of numbers.

1. 5, 2, 10

2. 5, 10, 50

3. 2, 3, 6

4. 5, 8, 40

Problems

Brain-teaser

Jim shares 15 biscuits equally between five plates. Jim writes a number sentence for the sharing. $15 \div 5 = 3$. Write a multiplication number sentence to show that the answer is correct. $? \times ? = ?$

Fractions of shapes

This square is cut into two equal pieces.
Each of these is worth one half.

$\frac{1}{2}$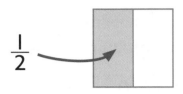

This square is divided into four equal pieces.
Each of these is worth one quarter.

$\frac{1}{4}$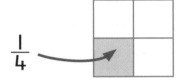

Look at the square cut into quarters.
We write this like this. $\frac{1}{4}$

- So one square is $\frac{1}{4}$ or one out of four.
- Two squares are $\frac{2}{4}$ or two out of four.
- Three squares are $\frac{3}{4}$ or three out of four.
- Four pieces of the square make a whole one.

This cake has been cut into three equal slices.
One slice of cake is a third of the cake, or $\frac{1}{3}$.
If you eat all the cake, you have eaten a whole one.

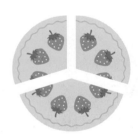

There are four equal pieces in this pizza.
Sophia takes one of the four pieces.
That is a quarter or $\frac{1}{4}$.

✓ Tip

The bottom number in a fraction tells you how many
equal parts the shape has been divided into. The top
number tells you how many of the parts to take.

Here is a rectangle.
Count how many equal pieces there are altogether.
Now count how many pieces have been shaded.
Say it as a fraction to a partner.

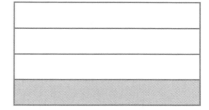

Here is a square.
Count how many equal pieces there are.
Now count how many equal pieces have been shaded.
Can you say the fractions that is unshaded?

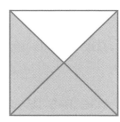

Activities

Write the fraction that has been shaded for each of these shapes.

1. 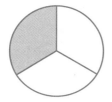   2. 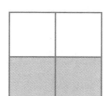   3. 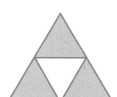   4.

Problems

Brain-teaser

Paul draws a rectangle. He draws lines to make four equal small rectangles inside his rectangle. He shades in two small rectangles. What fraction has Paul shaded?

Brain-buster

Martha bought a pizza for supper for her and Tom. Martha cut the pizza into four equal slices. She ate one slice. Tom ate two slices. What fraction of the pizza was left?

Finding fractions of numbers and quantities

Remember

$\frac{1}{2}$ means one half or one out of two equal pieces.

$\frac{1}{3}$ means one third or one out of three equal pieces.

$\frac{1}{4}$ means one quarter or one out of four equal pieces.

$\frac{2}{4}$ means two quarters or two out of four equal pieces.

$\frac{3}{4}$ means three quarters or three out of four equal pieces.

> ✓ **Tip**
>
> Use your multiplication tables to help you with fractions.
> $\frac{1}{2}$ of 6 is 3. Think about $3 \times 2 = 6$ and $6 \div 2 = 3$.

Here is a stick.
This stick is 20cm long.
Half of the stick is 10cm long.
$\frac{1}{2}$ of 20cm = 10cm

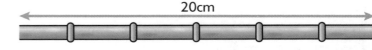

20cm

Use these stars to help you. Count the stars.
How many groups of two stars can you make?
4 groups. So one group of two is $\frac{1}{4}$ of the stars.
$\frac{1}{4}$ of 8 is 2. How many is $\frac{2}{4}$ of the stars?
How many is $\frac{3}{4}$ of the stars?

$\frac{2}{4}$ of 8 is 4.  $\frac{3}{4}$ of 8 is 6.

Talk maths

Here is an array of 12 dots.
Discuss the answers to these questions with your partner.

How many is $\frac{1}{4}$ of the dots?

How many is $\frac{1}{3}$ of the dots?

How many is $\frac{3}{4}$ of the dots?

Activities

Copy and complete these questions. You may find it helpful to draw some dots to help you to work out the answers.

1. $\frac{1}{2}$ of 10   2. $\frac{1}{4}$ of 8   3. $\frac{2}{4}$ of 16   4. $\frac{3}{4}$ of 16

Problems

Brain-teaser

Sandeep cuts off $\frac{1}{4}$ of a 24cm piece of tape. Write a fraction number sentence to show how much Sandeep cut.

Brain-buster

Lalita chooses a pencil that is 18cm long. Her naughty brother keeps sharpening the pencil until there is 12cm left. What fraction of the pencil has gone?

Recognising that $\frac{2}{4}$ is equivalent to $\frac{1}{2}$

Learn

Look at this square. It is divided into two equal parts.
So these are each worth half or $\frac{1}{2}$.

This square has been divided into quarters.
There are four quarters.
Each part is one quarter or $\frac{1}{4}$.

The two quarters and the half take
up the same amount of room.
They are equal. So $\frac{2}{4} = \frac{1}{2}$.

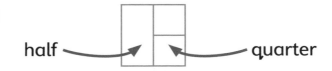
half — quarter

$\frac{1}{4}$ of 12 is 3.

$\frac{2}{4}$ of 12 is 6.

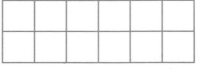

This rectangle is made from 12 squares.

$\frac{1}{2}$ of 12 is 6.

$\frac{2}{4}$ and $\frac{1}{2}$ are the same amount.

This pencil is 16cm long. Can you work out:

$\frac{1}{4}$ of 16

$\frac{2}{4}$ of 16

4, 8, 8. $\frac{2}{4}$ and $\frac{1}{2}$ are the same.

$\frac{1}{2}$ of 16

What do you notice about $\frac{2}{4}$ and $\frac{1}{2}$?

16cm

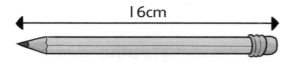

✓ Tip

If you split something in half the two pieces must be the same size. If you split something into quarters, each of the four pieces must be the same size.

Talk maths

Work with a partner to draw different-sized rectangles and squares on squared paper and divide them into fractions. Try drawing some that have 20 small squares in them.

What can you learn?

Activities

1. What is $\frac{1}{4}$ of 20? What is $\frac{2}{4}$ of 20? So what is $\frac{1}{2}$ of 20?

2. How much is $\frac{1}{4}$ of 8kg? How much is $\frac{2}{4}$ of 8kg? So how much is $\frac{1}{2}$ of 8kg?

3. How much is $\frac{1}{4}$ of 24cm? How much is $\frac{2}{4}$ of 24cm? So how much is $\frac{1}{2}$ of 24cm?

Problems

Brain-teaser

Jonas has a small bag of gravel. It weighs 16kg. How much does $\frac{1}{4}$ of the bag weigh? So how much will $\frac{1}{2}$ of the bag weigh?

Brain-buster

Jonas has a bucket of water with 12 litres in it. He pours out $\frac{1}{4}$ of the water. Then he pours out another $\frac{1}{4}$ of the water. What fraction of the water is left in the bucket? How many litres are left in the bucket?

Comparing and ordering measurements

Learn

We measure length using units.

These are the short ways of writing units of measures.

centimetre → cm   kilogram → kg   gram → g

metre → m   millilitre → ml   litre → l

This toy is 7cm tall.

Measurements can be ordered and compared using <, > or =.

Decide which is longer.

30cm > 20cm

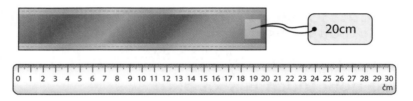

20cm

Decide which is lighter.

$1\frac{1}{2}$ kg < 3kg

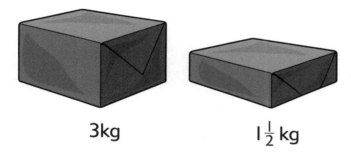

3kg $1\frac{1}{2}$ kg

Decide which container contains more liquid.

5l > 2l

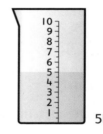 5l    2l

Scale A shows weighing in grams. The mass is 50g.

Scale B shows weighing in kilograms. The mass is 2kg.

 A    B

✓ **Tip**

Always make sure that the measurements are in the same unit.

Talk maths

Look at these three lengths.

| 50cm | 90cm | 40cm |

Look at the tens numbers to find the largest.

The order will be 90cm, 50cm and 40cm.

Start with the units. Are they all the same?

Discuss with a partner how you could order them from shortest to longest.

Do this again with these weights.

| 500g | 950g | 600g |

Look at the hundred digit this time. The order is 500g, 600g and 950g.

They are all in grams.

Here are some measurements in litres.

| $\frac{1}{2}$ litre | 3 litres | $2\frac{1}{2}$ litres |

Activities

1. **Copy these measures and add < or > to show which is larger.**
   a. 20km ? 25km.   b. $1\frac{1}{2}$ litres ? $\frac{1}{2}$ litres

2. **Now write these measures in order. Start with the smallest.**
   a. 55cm, 45cm, 48cm   b. 6kg, 5kg, 4kg   c. 3 litres, 4 litres, $3\frac{1}{2}$ litres

Problems

Brain-teaser

Tania has a 30cm ruler. Sophy has a 25cm ruler.
Who has the longer ruler?

Brain-buster

Tom and Tania are using sticky tape on a birthday gift. Tom uses 15cm of tape. Tania uses 17cm of tape. Who uses more tape?

Cindy buys two bags of sweets that each weighs 40g. Sacha buys 60g of sweets. Who has the heavier sweets?

Choosing and using standard units

Learn

Mass is measured in kilograms and grams.
Capacity is measured in litres and millilitres.
Temperature is measured in degrees Celsius. We write °C.
Lengths are measured in metres and centimetres.

Before you measure something make an estimate and write it down.
Use your eyes.

- How long does something look?
- How high is the water in the jug?
- How much do you think that is?
- Pick up the item to be weighed.
- How heavy does it feel to you?

✓ Tip

Check the scale before making a reading.
Decide what the reading is halfway between each number.

Look at these measuring tools.
The scale is marked in 100g from 0g to 1kg.
So it increases by 100g each time.
What mass does this show?

600g, 500l, 15cm, 23°

The scale is marked in 100ml.
So it increases by 100ml each time.
How much is in the jug?

The scale is marked in 1cm.
So it increases by 1cm each time.
What length does the arrow show?

The scale is marked in 2°C. So it increases by 2°C each time.
The little line in between marks the next 1°C. What temperature is shown?

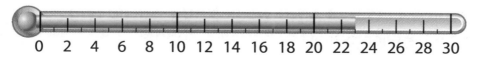

Talk maths

Look at the scales below.
Talk with a partner about the different scales.
What unit is shown on each scale?
Read each scale. What measurement
does it show?

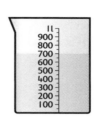  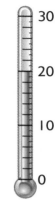

Activities

Here are some measuring tools.

1. **What is the length shown on the ruler?**

2. **What is the weight shown on the weighing scales?**

3. **How much is in the jug?**

4. **What is the temperature on the thermometer?**

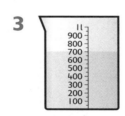 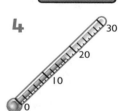

Problems

Brain-teaser

This thermometer shows the morning
temperature and the afternoon temperature.
How much warmer was it in the afternoon than in the morning?

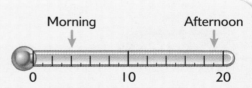

Brain-buster

Marc weighed out the same amount of butter, flour and
sugar. The scale shows how heavy the butter was.
What was the total weight of the butter, flour and sugar?

Telling the time

Learn

The short hand points to the hour.

The long hand points to how many minutes.

This clock shows 9 hours and 0 minutes.

The time is 9 o'clock.

When the minute hand points to 12 it means o'clock.

Count the minutes in 5s.

Start at 12.

Count around the clock in 5s for the minutes.

You counted 60 minutes.

Up to 30 minutes we say 5 past, 10 past, quarter past, 20 past, 25 past the hour.

Then we say 25 to, 20 to, quarter to, 10 to and 5 to the next hour.

When the longer hand points to 6, that is 30 minutes past, or half past the hour.

✓ Tip

Times past the hour: look at the number that the hour hand has just passed.

Times to the hour: look at the number that the hour hand will get to next.

What time does this clock say? 7.40

Talk maths

Look at this clock.
Talk with a partner.
Discuss what time you think this clock shows.
Can you explain why?

What time does this clock show?

How many minutes to 6 is it?

Activities

Draw the hands on a clock face for each of these times.

1. **Quarter past seven**

2. **Quarter to three**

3. **Five past two**

4. **Twenty past nine**

5. **Twenty-five to ten**

Problems

Brain-teaser

Jamie arrives at school at ten to nine.
Draw the hands on a clock face to show this time.

Brain-buster

These clocks show what time Jan leaves home
and what time she arrives at the library.

How many minutes does her journey take?

Leaves home   Arrives at library

Comparing and sequencing time

Learn

There are 7 days in a week.
An hour has 60 minutes.

Remember these facts.

Count round the clock from 12 and back again in 5s.
You should count to 60. That is the number of minutes in an hour.

Look at these two clocks.
Clock A shows 5 o'clock.
Clock B shows 10 minutes past 5.
To work out the time difference between the two clocks count on in 5 minutes from 5 o'clock to 10 past 5.
This gives a count of 5, then 10.
So 10 minutes has passed.

A

B

Look at these two clocks.
Clock C shows 10 minutes past 3.
Clock D shows 20 minutes to 4.
To find the difference in time between the two clocks count on in minutes from the 10 minutes past to the 20 minutes to time.

C

D

This clock face shows the position of the two minute hands shown on clocks C and D.
Count in 5s. 5, 10, 15, 20, 25, 30.
So the difference between the two times is 30 minutes.

Talk maths

Clock E shows 20 minutes past 8.
How many minutes is it until 20 minutes to 9?

Clock F shows 10 minutes to 5.
How many minutes is it until quarter past 5?

Point with your
finger and
count in 5s.

10 minutes to 5 o'clock: 5, 10.
5 o'clock to quarter past 5: 15, 20, 25.
The time difference is 25 minutes.

Activities

1. Which clock shows the earlier time?

2. Which clock shows the later time?

3. Which clock shows a half past time?

4. Which clock shows a quarter to time?

5. How many minutes are there from the clock G time to the clock H time?

Problems

Brain-teaser

Mark leaves for school at half past eight.
He gets to school at five minutes to nine.
How long does it take Mark to get to school?

Brain-buster

Sum Mei does her maths homework from five past four to half past four.
She then does her English homework from half past four until ten to five.
Which homework takes longer? How many minutes longer?

Money

Learn

Here are the coins we use.

✓ Tip

To write an amount of money less than £1, write the p sign after the price, like this.

To write an amount of money in pounds, the £ sign goes before the price, like this.

Different ways of making 50p.

  This is a 50p coin.

    20p + 20p + 10p makes 50p.

This is another way to make 50p.

Use coins to help you to find the total.

When finding the cost of two items begin by adding the tens then the ones. Try this.

21p + 32p = 20p + 30p + 1p + 2p = 50p + 3p = 53p

21p

32p

Talk maths

Say the value of each coin. Then total them.

Talk with a partner about the easiest way to add these coins.

Always start with the largest value and end with the smallest... so 10p add 5p add 2p is 17p.

50p add 10p is 60p. Then add the smallest value coin. 60p add 5p is 65p.

£2 and £1 is £3. Then add the pence coins. £3 add 50p add 20p is £3 and 70p.

Activities

1. Write a coin number sentence that totals 15p.

2. Which coins could you use to make a total of 22p?

3. Write a coin number sentence that totals 45p.

Problems

Brain-teaser

Lara buys a key ring for 75p. Write a coin number sentence to total 75p. Use as few coins as possible.

Brain-buster

Find three different ways of making £1 using coins. Write a number sentence for each one.

Solving money problems

Learn

Tom spends 13p. How much change does he get from 20p?

There are two ways to solve this.
Count up from 13 to 20 as if you are giving change:
13 to 15 is 2.
Then 15 to 20 is 5. So that is 2 + 5 is 7.
The change is 7p.
Or take 13 away from 20 by counting back.

You decide which method you like.

Now try these.

Tom buys a pen for 12p and a notebook for 5p.
How much change will he have from 20p?

12p and 5p is 17p. Counting up to 20p is another 3p. So Tom has 3p change.

Sarah buys a comic for 32p and a pen for 16p.
How much change does she have from 50p?

One way to do this is to add 10p then 6p. So 32p add 10p is 42p and add 6p is 48p. So Sarah gets 2p change.

You can write this out as an addition sentence like this.
32 + 16 = 32 + 10 + 6 = 42 + 6 = 48
50 − 48 = 2.
So the change is 2p.

✓ Tip

To solve some money problems, you may want to work mentally.
It can be helpful to add the tens digits first and then the ones.

Talk maths

Count up to work out the change with a partner.

16p ⟶

13p ⟶

37p ⟶

```
 0  1  2  3  4  5  6  7  8  9  10  11  12  13  14  15  16  17  18  19  20
```

Activities

Write the total.

1. 23p + 16p
2. 38p + 19p

Write the change.

3. 20p − 16p
4. 50p − 29p

Problems

Brain-teaser

Pip spends 3p on a chew and 9p on a lolly.
How much change does Pip receive from 20p?

Brain-buster

Mina buys two notepads at 24p each and a pen for 47p.
How much change does Mina receive from £1?

Comparing and sorting 2D shapes

Learn

 circle

 triangle

 square

 rectangle

hexagon   pentagon   octagon   semicircle

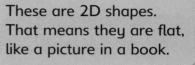
These are 2D shapes. That means they are flat, like a picture in a book.

	Number of sides	Number of vertices
Triangle	3	3
Square	4	4
Rectangle	4	4
Pentagon	5	5
Hexagon	6	6
Octagon	8	8

A corner on a shape is called a **vertex**. Two or more are called **vertices**.

vertex

What do you notice about the number of sides and the number of vertices? For these shapes, these numbers are the same.

The circle is different. It has one side and no vertices.

Some shapes have a line of symmetry. Look at this shape.

This rectangle has a line of symmetry.

One side of the line is a mirror image of the other.

✓ Tip

If you need help with symmetry, use a mirror to check. Put the mirror on the line. Look in the mirror. What can you see?

Talk maths

Let's look at this triangle. The line goes through the middle of the triangle. What you see one side of the line is a mirror image of what is on the other side of the line.

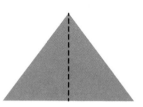

If you are not sure whether there is a line of symmetry, draw the shape carefully onto some paper. Cut it out. Now try folding to see if you can find a line of symmetry.

Another way is to use a mirror like this.
Look in the mirror. If what you see is the rest of the shape then you have found a line of symmetry.

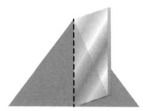

How would you explain to someone how to find out whether there is a line of symmetry for the rectangle?

Activities

1. How many sides does a pentagon have? How many does an octagon have?

2. How many vertices does an octagon have? How many does a hexagon have?

3. Which shapes have curved sides?

Problems

Brain-teaser
This is a hexagon. Copy it and draw a line of symmetry.

Brain-buster
Here is a four-sided shape. It is not a square and it is not a rectangle. Does it have a line of symmetry?

Comparing and sorting 3D shapes

Learn

 cone   cylinder   triangular prism   pyramid (square based)

 sphere pentagonal prism cube   cuboid

These are 3D shapes. That means they are solid.

A face is a side of a 3D shape. An edge is the line where two faces meet.

face — edge — vertex

Look at these shapes. Think about the parts of the shapes that are hidden in the pictures.

A vertex is where two straight edges meet. Two or more are called vertices.

How many vertices, faces and edges does each shape have? We can write these into the table.

Shape	Number of vertices	Number of faces	Number of edges
Cone	0	2	1
Cylinder	0	3	2
Triangular prism	6	5	9
Square-based pyramid	5	5	8

✓ Tip

In a picture you cannot see all of the 3D shape. Find an object that you can pick up if you are stuck. For example, a cereal pack is a cuboid, and a can of beans is a cylinder.

Talk maths

Look around you. What 3D shapes can you find?

A shoe box is a good example of a cuboid. You may find a cylinder in a food cupboard. It could be a tin of food or a packet of biscuits.

I counted 6 faces, 8 vertices and 12 edges.

Can you find anything that is cone shaped?
Perhaps you have some building bricks that you could use?

Discuss each shape that you find. How many faces, vertices and edges does each shape have?

Activities

1. **Use the shape pictures to help you to answer these questions.**

   a. Which shapes have curved faces?

   b. Which shape has the most edges?

   c. How many vertices does the cone have?

Problems

Brain-teaser
Myla says that the two 3D shapes she chose have five faces in total. Which two shapes do you think she chose?

Brain-buster
Mark has a shape that has five faces and another shape with nine edges. Which two shapes do you think he chose?

Recognising 2D shapes on the surface of 3D shapes

Learn

Here are some 3D shapes. Look at the different shapes that can be seen on these shapes. Look for circles, squares and triangles.

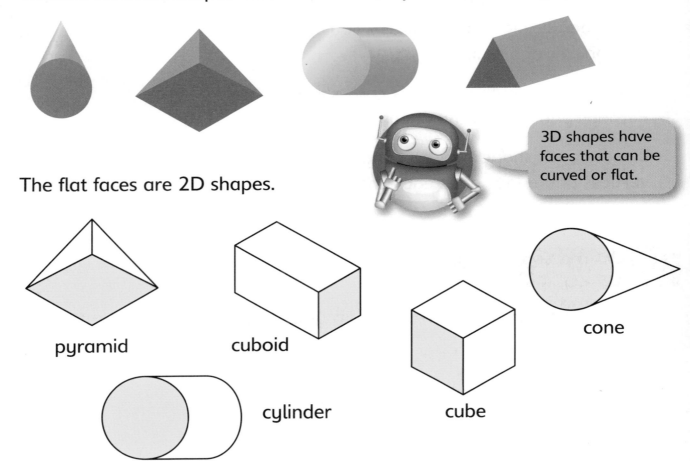

The flat faces are 2D shapes.

3D shapes have faces that can be curved or flat.

pyramid

cuboid

cone

cylinder

cube

Look at the pyramid. It has a square for its base and a triangle for the other faces.

Now look at the cylinder. It has a circle face at each end. Its other face is curved.

The cone has a circle for its base. Its other face curves up to a point.

The cube has six square faces. Each face is exactly the same as the other five.

The cuboid has rectangles as some of its faces.

Talk maths

Work with a partner. Discuss the 3D shapes that you know. Can you think of an example of a 3D shape that has only square faces? Which shapes have rectangles on some faces?

Some 3D shapes have opposite faces that are all the same.

Activities

Think about things around you.

1. Name something that has a circle for a face.

2. Name something that has a rectangle for a face.

3. Name something that has a triangle for a face.

Problems

Brain-teaser

Steve builds a model with some building bricks. He chooses some shapes with two circle faces. He chooses other shapes with three rectangle faces and two triangle faces. Which shapes did he choose?

Brain-buster

Sally builds a model too. She chooses shapes that have two triangle faces but five faces altogether. She chooses some more shapes with one square face. She also chooses some shapes that have just one circle face. Which shapes does she choose?

Patterns and sequences

Do you have wallpaper at home? Does it have a pattern? Look at this piece of wallpaper. This is a repeating pattern.

Say this repeating pattern.

A repeating pattern like this has the same items in the same order. This is repeated each time.

Look carefully at this arrangement.

It is a repeating pattern. The pattern is triangle rectangle rectangle. That pattern repeats.
Say this pattern.

The pattern is: square triangle circle. This pattern can repeat again and again.

✓ Tip

Saying the pattern aloud helps you to see that it repeats.

Talk maths

Say these pattern beginnings.
Say what comes next.

Activities

1. Copy and complete the pattern for two repeats.

2. Copy and complete this pattern for two repeats.

Copy these patterns. ✔ them if they repeat correctly. Put a ✗ if not correct.

3.

4.

5.

Problems

Brain-teaser
John makes this pattern. Draw the next four shapes.

Brain-buster
Jenny draws this pattern. What is missing?

Position, direction and movement

If Jo makes a quarter turn, she will face the car. If she makes a half turn, she will face the book. If she makes a three-quarter turn, she will face the drum. If she makes a whole turn, she will face the teddy.

Look at the two clocks. On the second clock the minute hand has turned through a right angle. A right angle is a quarter turn.

The minute hand of a clock moves to make a half turn, or two right angles.

And the hand turns through another right angle to show a three-quarter turn.

When the clock shows 10 o'clock the minute hand has turned through 4 right angles. It has made a full turn.

Now look at these two pictures.

Sam has walked along the road in a straight line.

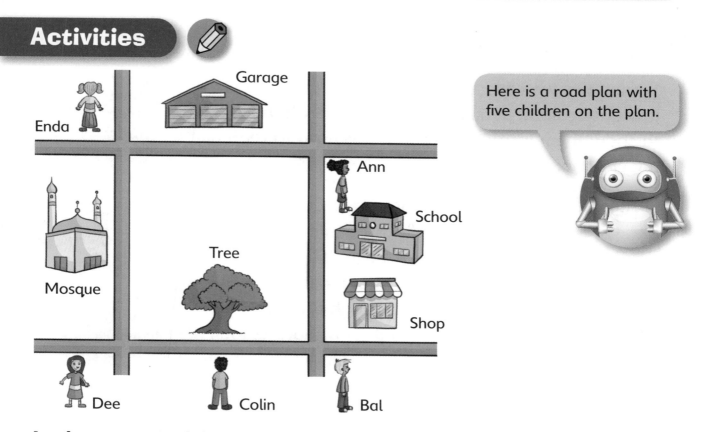

Here is a road plan with five children on the plan.

1. **Ann turns a right angle to the right. What will she see?**

2. **Bal turns a right angle anticlockwise. What will he see?**

3. **Colin crosses the road and walks straight ahead. What will he see?**

4. **Dee turns two right angles clockwise. What will she see?**

5. **Enda turns anticlockwise through three right angles. What will she see?**

Problems

Brain-teaser

Draw the route James takes to school. He leaves his house and turns left one right angle. He walks along the road to the crossroads. He turns left again. His school is there.

Interpreting and making simple data charts

Learn

Sometimes we collect information about things like favourite colour, pets, holidays. We need to have a way to show the information so that it is easy to read and understand.

All these charts show the same information about the children's favourite colours.

Tally chart

Colour	Tally
Blue	ЩЩ II
Red	ЩЩ ЩЩ III
Yellow	ЩЩ I

Tallies are a quick way to collect the information. Look at the blue row. It has |||| to show 4, and then a line through for 5. Count the tallies for each colour.

There are 7 blue tallies.

Table

This table contains numbers. Compare it with the tally chart. You should find the same information.

Colour	Number of children
Blue	7
Red	13
Yellow	6

Pictogram

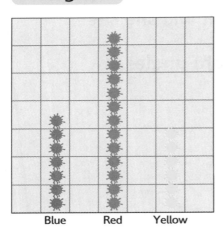

Blue   Red   Yellow

On the pictogram, one ✴ stands for one vote for a colour. Count the pictures for blue, red and yellow. Are these the same as in the tally chart? They should be!

Block chart

The block graph has a scale that goes up in 2s on the left-hand side. Compare the table and the block graph. They show the same information!

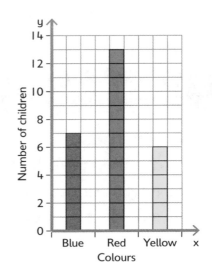

Talk maths

Look at the graphs and tables on page 68. Talk about how they are the same and how they are different. Which do you think is the best one for showing favourite colours?

Activities

Some children collected this information. Copy the table below and add the information to it.

Cats	Add your numbers here
Dogs	Add your numbers here
Rabbits	Add your numbers here
Mice	Add your numbers here

1. ||||| ||| children have cats as pets.

2. ||||| ||||| || children have dogs as pets.

3. ||||| || children have rabbits as pets.

4. |||| children have mice as pets.

5. Write a title for your table.

6. Draw a pictogram or block graph for the data.

Problems

Brain-teaser
Five more children buy mice. Which pet is least popular now?

Brain-buster
How many more children like cats and dogs than like rabbits?

Using and making charts

Learn

Graphs show you information with pictures, blocks, tallies or numbers.

Look at the block graph. Count the wins for Monday. How many games did Tom win on the other days?

Tom plays an online game against his friend. The block graph shows the number of times he won the game each day.

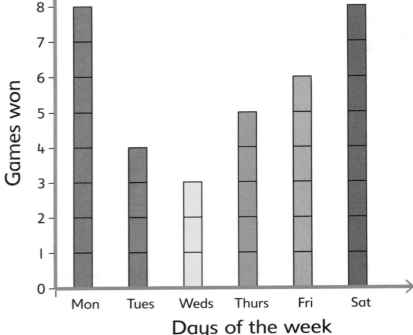

Activities

1. On which day did Tom win six games?

2. How many games did Tom win on Wednesday?

3. When did Tom win four games?

4. What was the score for Thursday?

5. On which two days did Tom win the same number of games?

Problems

Brain-teaser
Tom forgot that he had won another game on Wednesday. How many games did he win on Wednesday?

Making totals and comparisons

Learn

You can find information from a chart or diagram.

This block graph shows the colours of shoes worn by a class of children. The scale at the side goes up in 2s. Count the blocks for each colour.

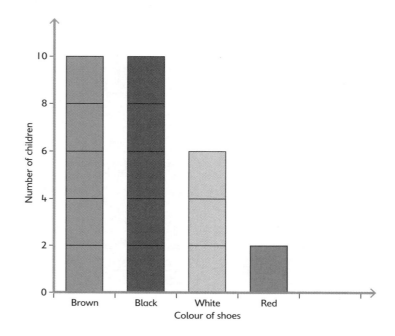

Activities

Use the block diagram to answer the questions.

1. Which two colours scored the same number?

2. How many pairs of shoes are there in total?

3. Five more children came into the classroom. They all wore blue shoes. Copy the graph and draw a column for the block diagram for the blue shoes.

4. How many more children wore black shoes than blue shoes?

Problems

Brain-buster

Which is more? The number of children wearing black shoes and red shoes, or the number of children wearing brown shoes and white shoes? How many more?

Multiplication table

x	1	2	3	4	5	6	7	8	9	10	11	12
1	1	2	3	4	5	6	7	8	9	10	11	12
2	2	4	6	8	10	12	14	16	18	20	22	24
3	3	6	9	12	15	18	21	24	27	30	33	36
4	4	8	12	16	20	24	28	32	36	40	44	48
5	5	10	15	20	25	30	35	40	45	50	55	60
6	6	12	18	24	30	36	42	48	54	60	66	72
7	7	14	21	28	35	42	49	56	63	70	77	84
8	8	16	24	32	40	48	56	64	72	80	88	96
9	9	18	27	36	45	54	63	72	81	90	99	108
10	10	20	30	40	50	60	70	80	90	100	110	120
11	11	22	33	44	55	66	77	88	99	110	121	132
12	12	24	36	48	60	72	84	96	108	120	132	144